Mary and Martha

WRITTEN BY Marty Rhodes Figley

ILLUSTRATED BY Cat Bowman Smith

WILLIAM B. EERDMANS PUBLISHING COMPANY

GRAND RAPIDS, MICHIGAN

For my sister Carol, with love — M.R.F.

To Vicki, Madeline, Dot, Kay, Gracie, and Mary — sisters all — C.B.S.

© 1995 Wm. B. Eerdmans Publishing Co.
255 Jefferson Ave., Grand Rapids, Michigan 49503

Printed in Hong Kong

00 99 98 97 96 95   7 6 5 4 3 2 1

Library of Congress Cataloging-in-Publication Data
Figley, Marty Rhodes, 1948 -
Mary and Martha / by Marty Figley; illustrated by Cat Bowman Smith.
p.   cm.
Summary: A retelling of the story of two very differnt sisters
and what they learned when Jesus visited their house.
ISBN 0-8028-5079-0
1. Mary, of Bethany, Saint — Juvenile literature.   2. Martha, Saint —
Juvenile literature.   3. Bible. N.T. Luke X, 38-43 — Biography — Juvenile literature.
4. Bible stories, English — N.T. Luke.   [1. Martha, Saint.   2. Mary, of Bethany, Saint.
3. Bible stories — N.T.]   I. Martha, Saint.   2. Mary, of Bethany, Saint.
3. Bible stories — N.T.]   I. Smith, Cat Bowman, ill.   II. Title.
Bs2490.M2F54   1995
226.4'09505 — dc20   95 - 5151
                              CIP
                              AC

Book design by Joy Chu

Martha and Mary were sisters who shared the same house. But they were as different as morning and evening.

Martha kept busy all the time.
She liked to shop at the market,
make spicy stews,
and bake fresh bread.

When she wasn't cooking,
Martha would scrub the floor,
wash the clothes,
and dust all the furniture.

Sometimes Martha worked so hard that she forgot to take a rest. Then she would get grumpy and out of sorts.

"Be quiet, be quiet!" she would yell to the children who played hide-and-seek in the shady courtyard.

Mary was not busy all the time.
She liked to think about ideas,
read interesting books,
strum her harp,
write letters to friends,
and play hide-and-seek
with the children in the shady
courtyard.

Sometimes Mary daydreamed so much that she forgot to do her household tasks. Then she would apologize to Martha. "I'm sorry, big sister. I'm sorry I forgot to buy pomegranates at the market."

"Oh, chicken feathers!" Martha would say in frustration. What was she going to do about Mary?

Jesus was a good friend of both
Martha and Mary.
He knew he was always
welcome at their house.
It was a place where he could
rest and relax.

One day Jesus came for a visit. He needed a rest from his preaching and teaching.

Martha was excited.
"I must make my spicy stew, bake fresh bread, cut slices of delicious honey cake, and fix a cozy place for Jesus to sleep tonight," she said, as she rushed around the house.

Mary was glad to see Jesus too. But she did not rush around the house.

Instead, she sat on the floor by Jesus' feet. He told her many wise and wonderful things, and her face shone as she listened.

Meanwhile, Martha got busier and busier.
But things weren't going well in the kitchen.
The spicy stew was burning.
The bread wasn't baking fast enough.
And Martha discovered that the honey cake
was gone: Mary had eaten it all for
breakfast.

   "Oh, chicken feathers!" exclaimed Martha.
What was she going to serve for dessert?

Worst of all, when Martha carried the heavy stewpot to the table, she almost tripped over Mary, who was still sitting at Jesus' feet. Martha was annoyed. She turned to Jesus and asked in a grumpy voice, "Why don't you tell Mary to help me with dinner? She's just sitting there doing nothing!"

Jesus smiled at Martha and made her sit down beside him.

"Martha," he said, "you're working too hard on the dinner. Your sister Mary is doing something very important. She has chosen to sit quietly and listen to my teachings. That is the better thing to do."

The next morning, after Jesus had left,
Mary went to the market with a list.
She came back with a brimming basket.
"Look at these beautiful pomegranates!"
she exclaimed to Martha.

Martha smiled but set the basket aside. "I'm sorry I was cross with you, Mary. And I'm sad that I missed hearing what Jesus told you, all those wise and wonderful things."

Mary hugged Martha and said, "You need a rest today, big sister. This morning you must let me cook and clean for you. Then I will tell you all the things that Jesus said."

Martha tried to stay inside and fold laundry.

But Mary was firm: "You need to get out of the house."

"Oh, chicken feathers!" Martha said, as usual—but she let Mary push her out of the door.

"Don't think about work," Mary said. "Have some fun! Go play hide-and-seek with the children in the shady courtyard."

And that's just what Martha did.